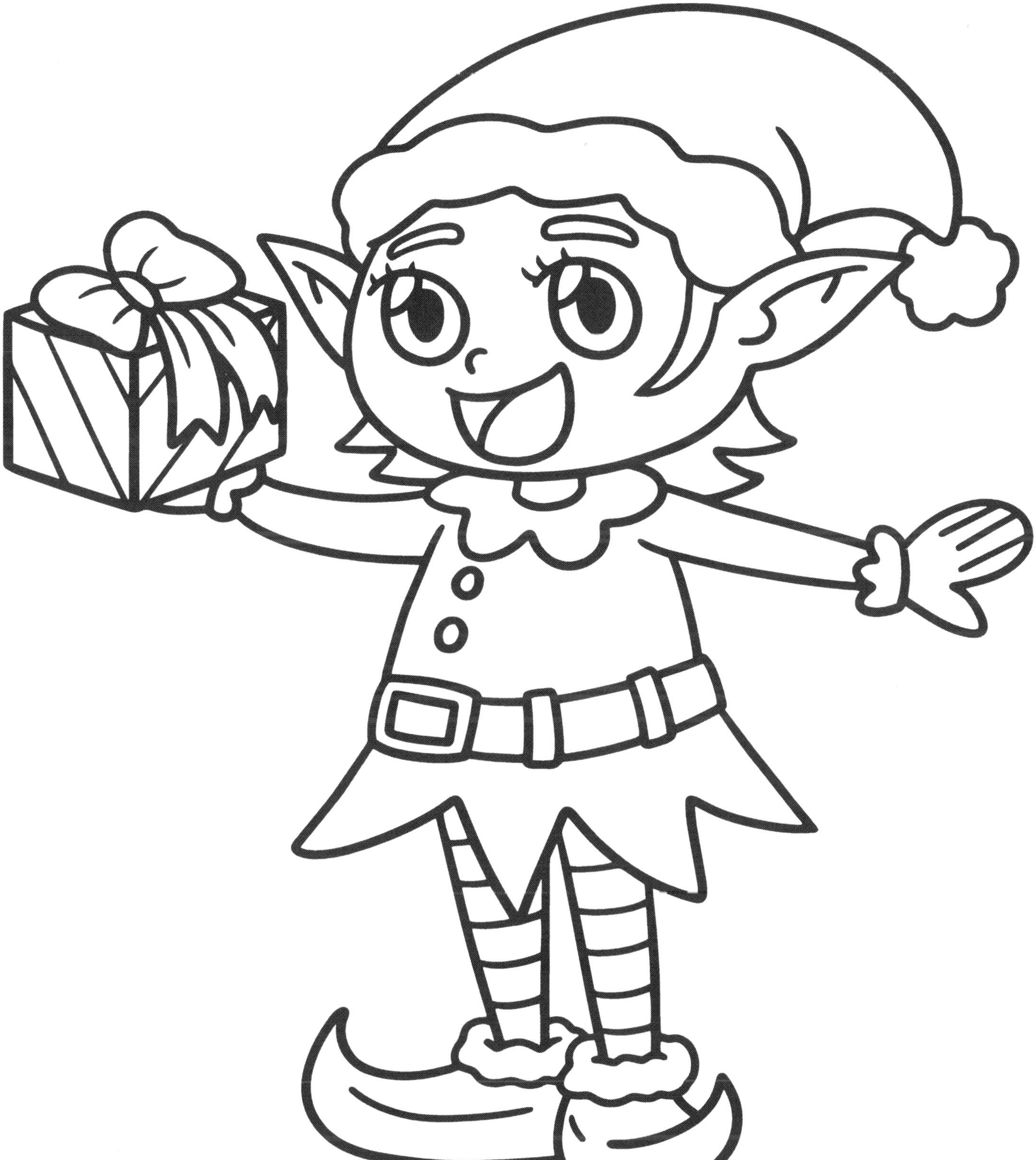

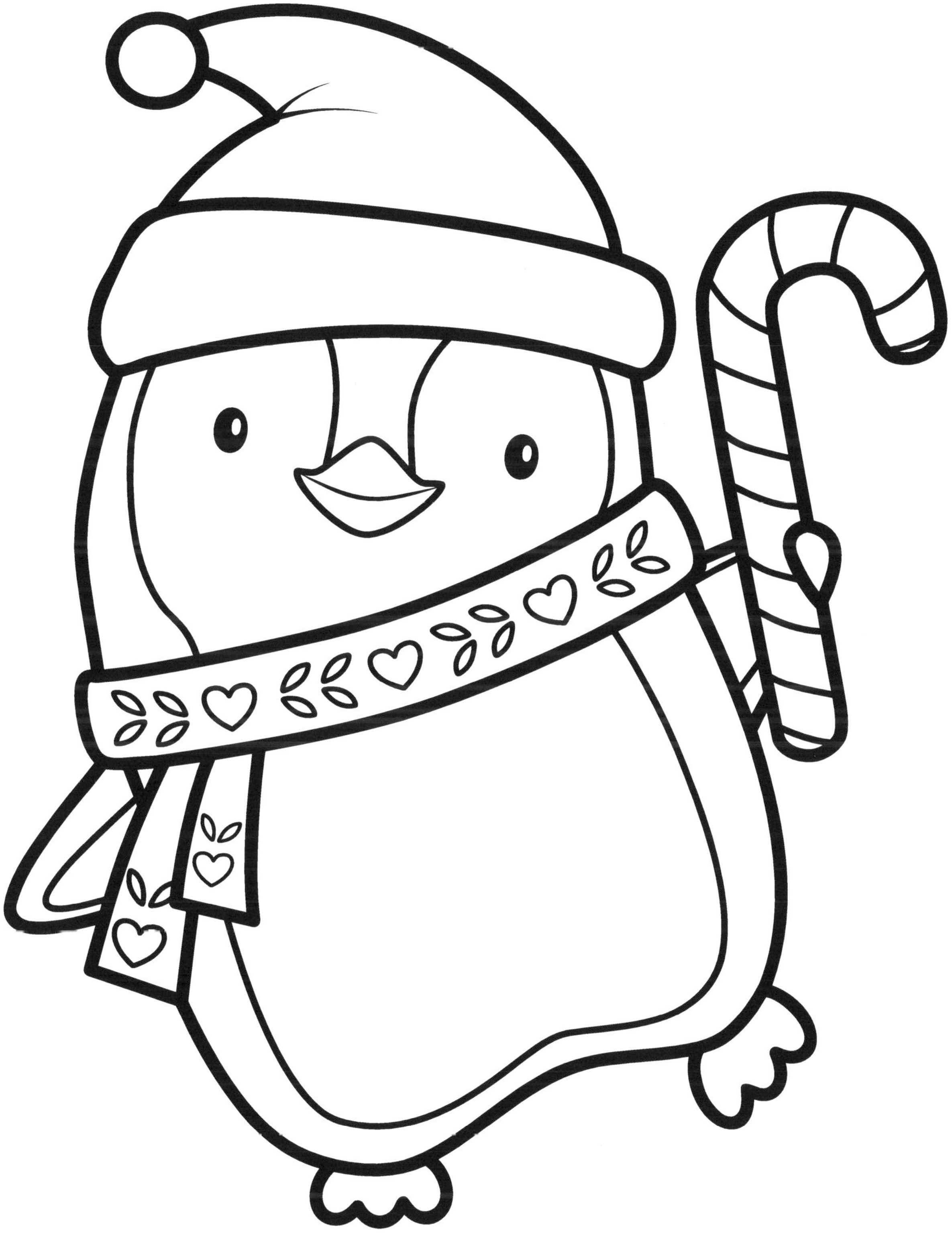

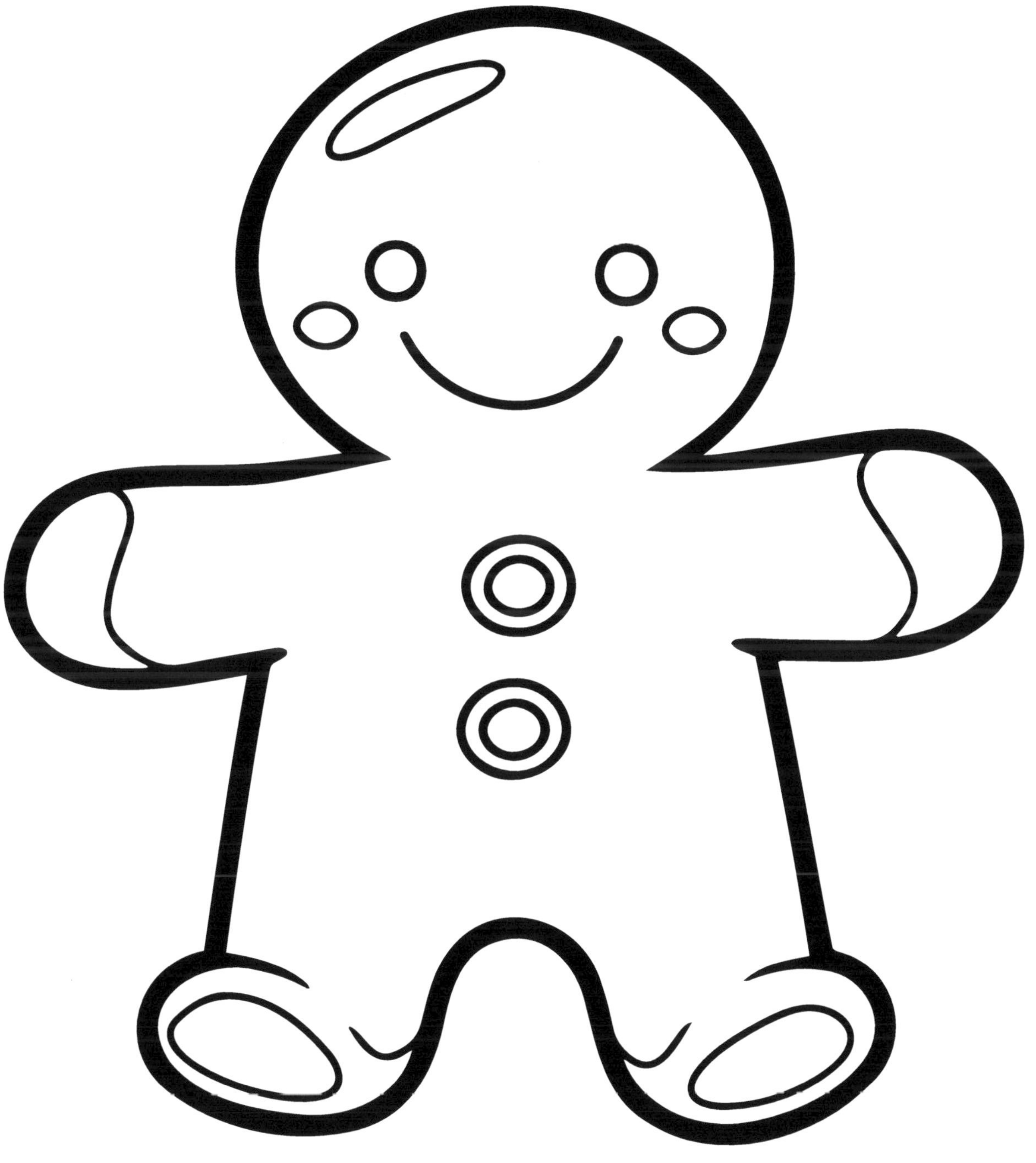

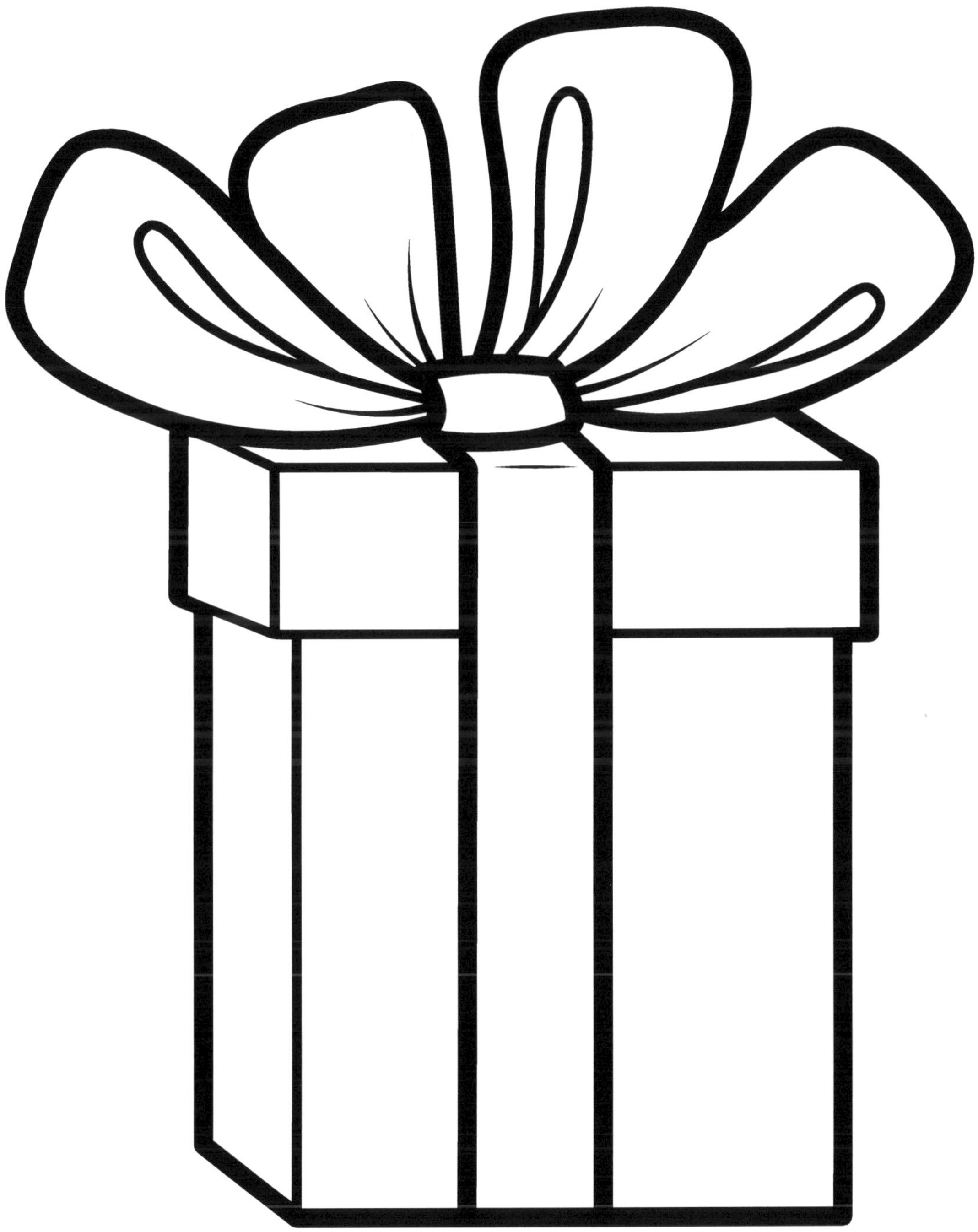

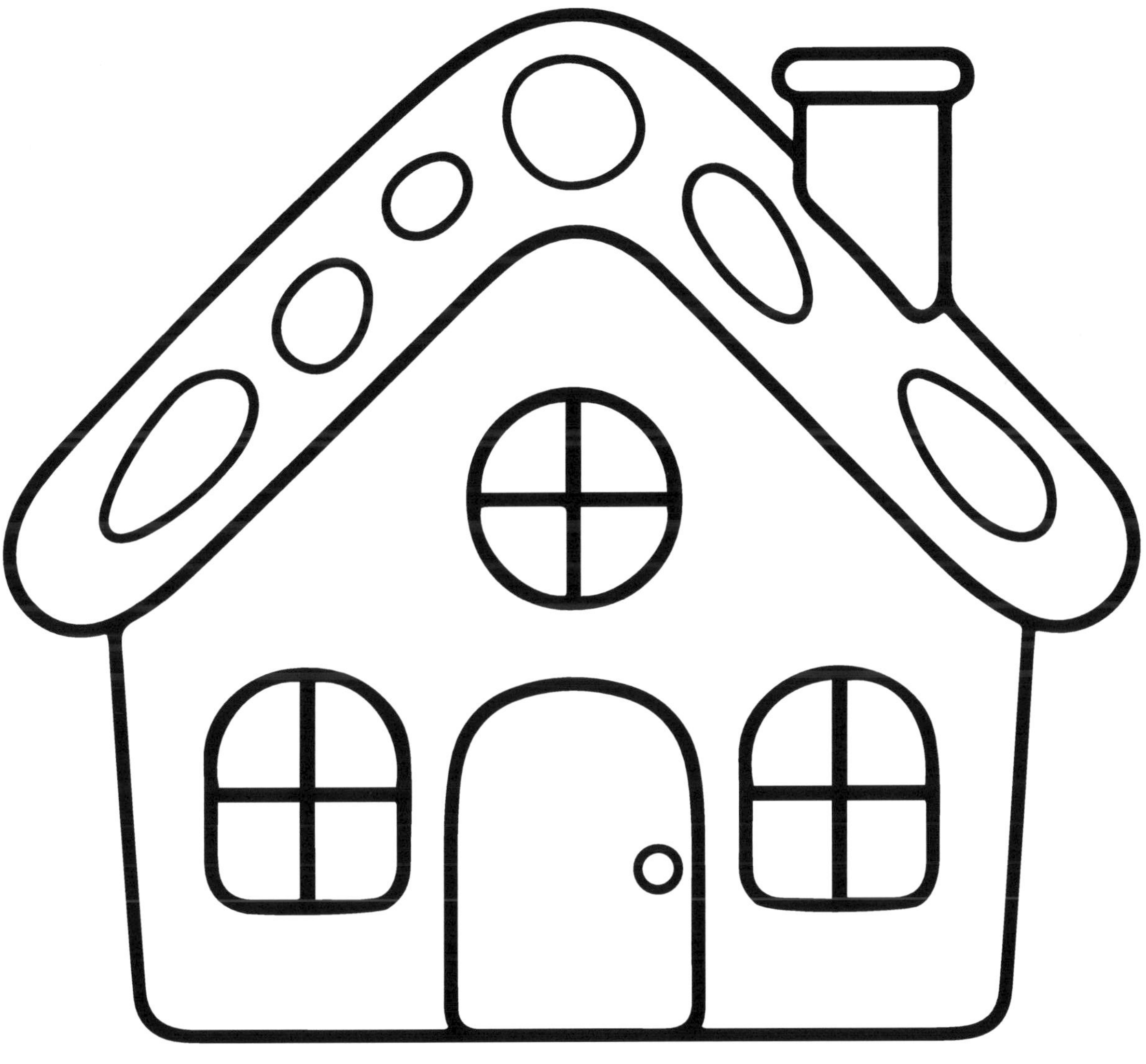

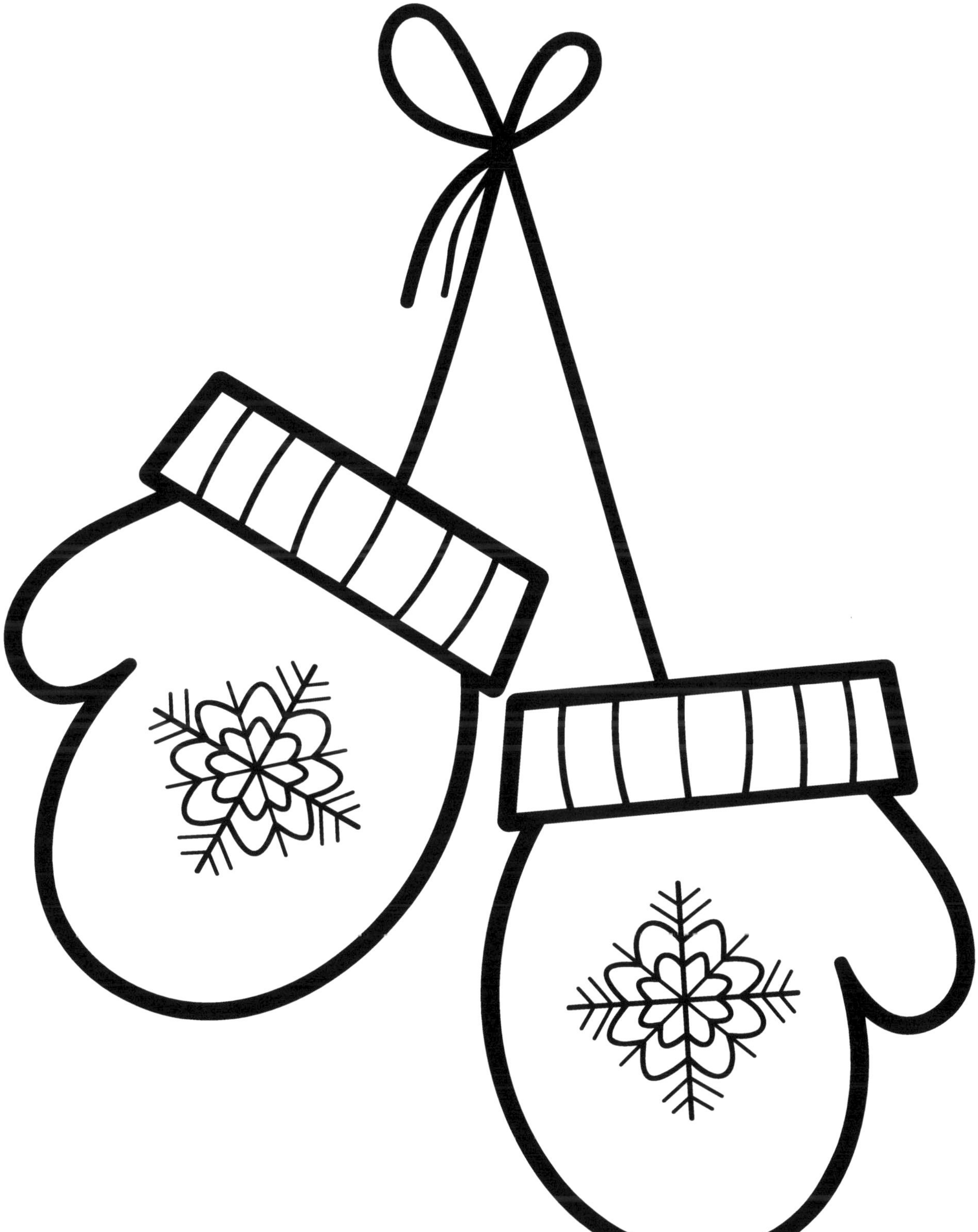

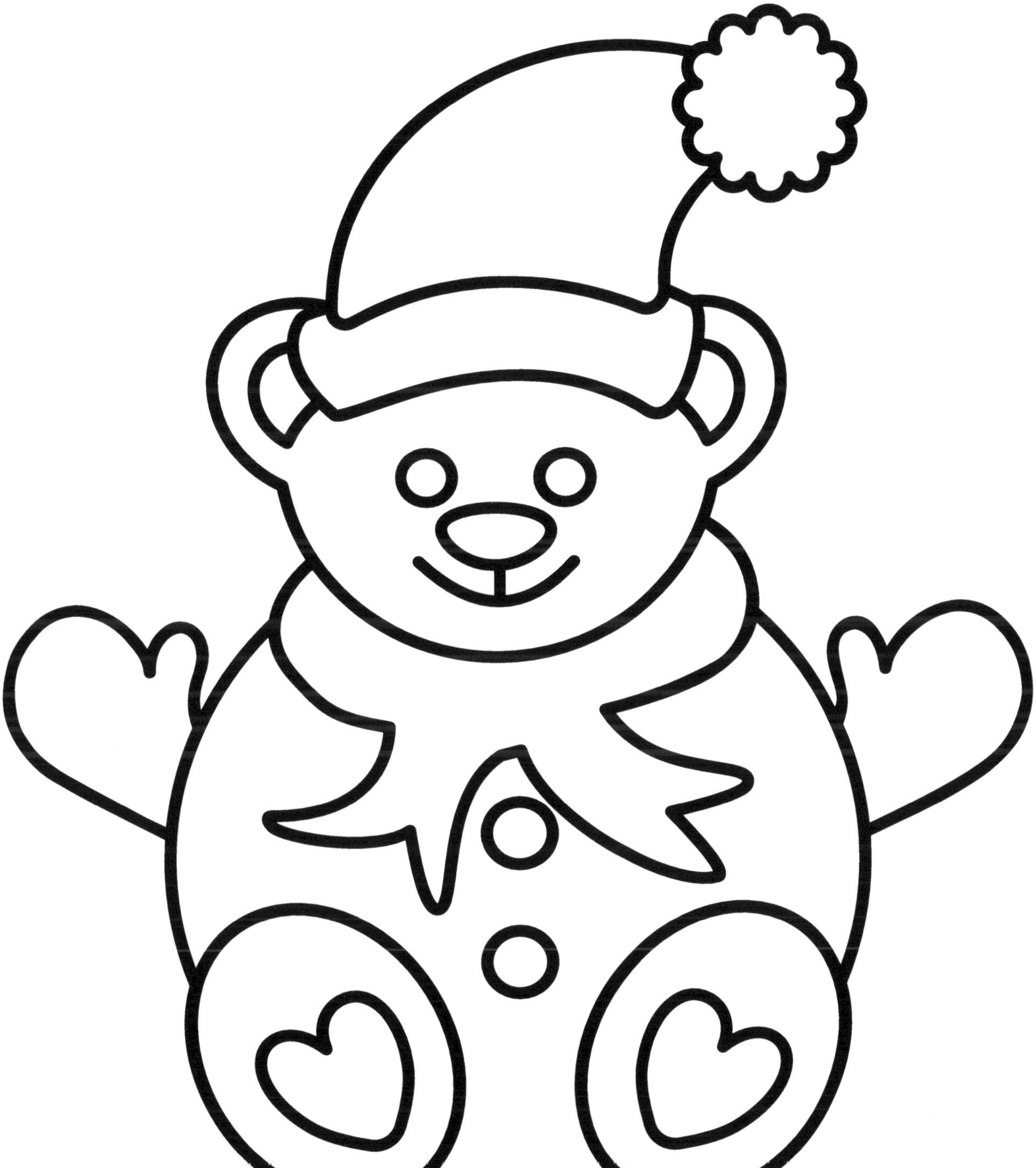

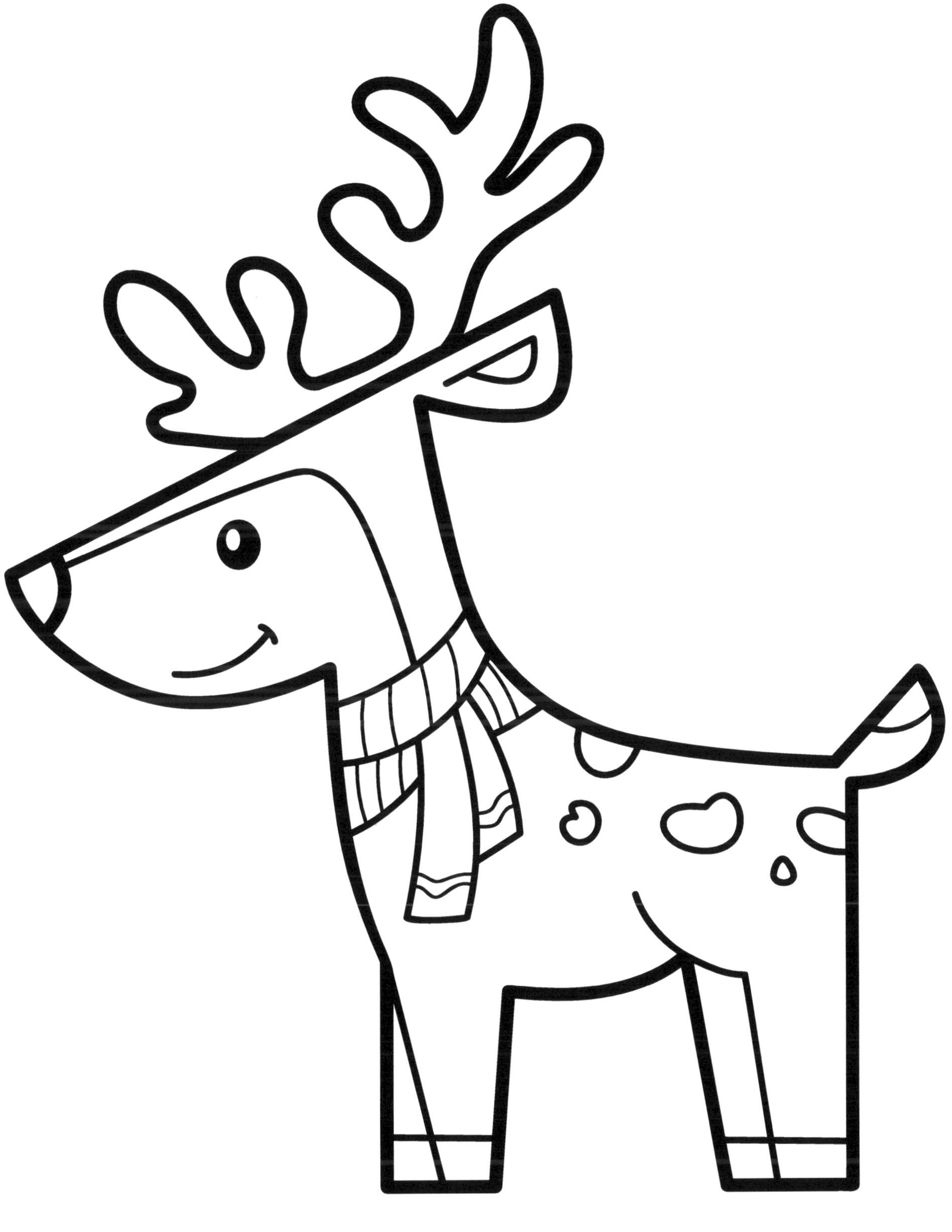

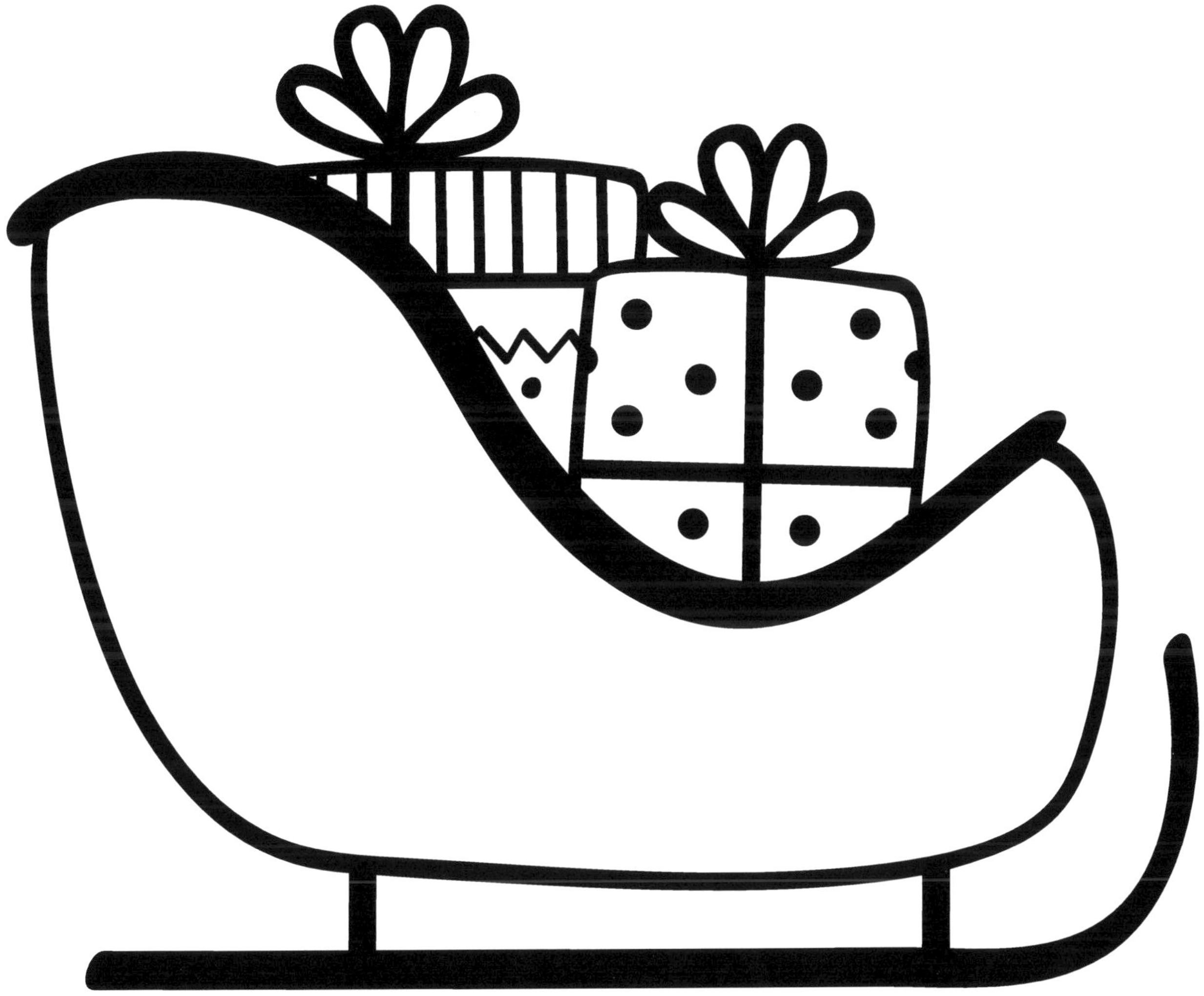

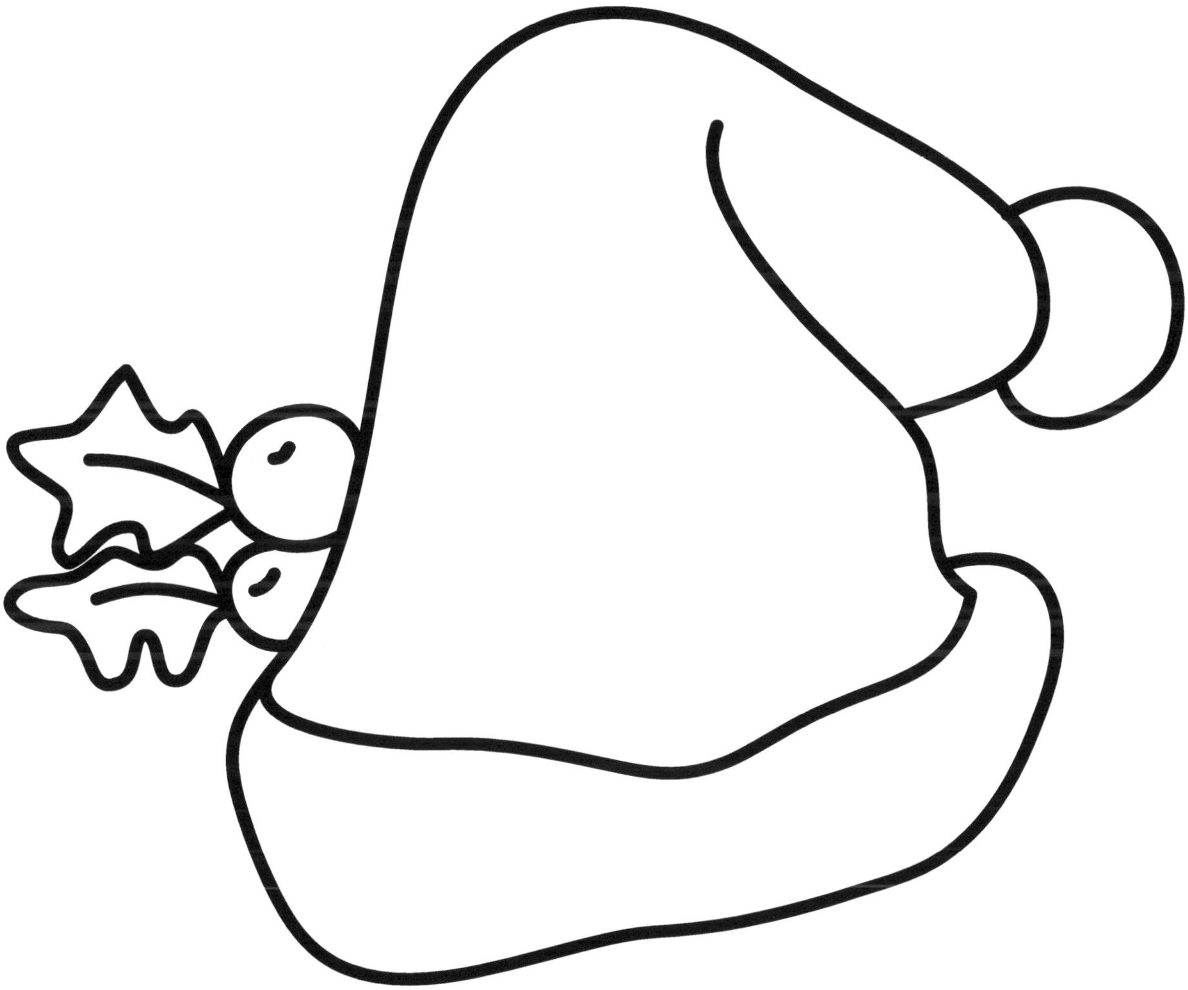

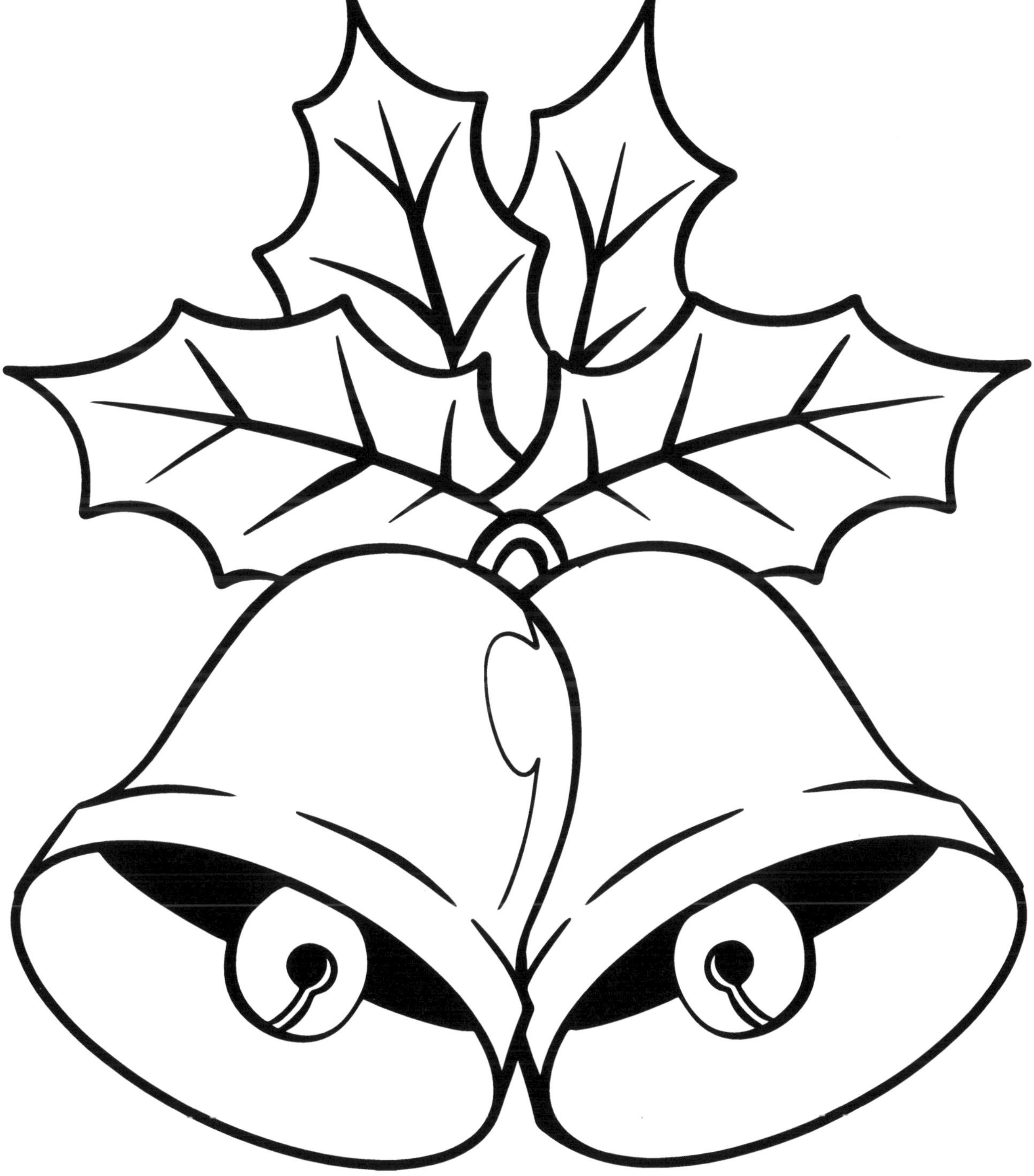

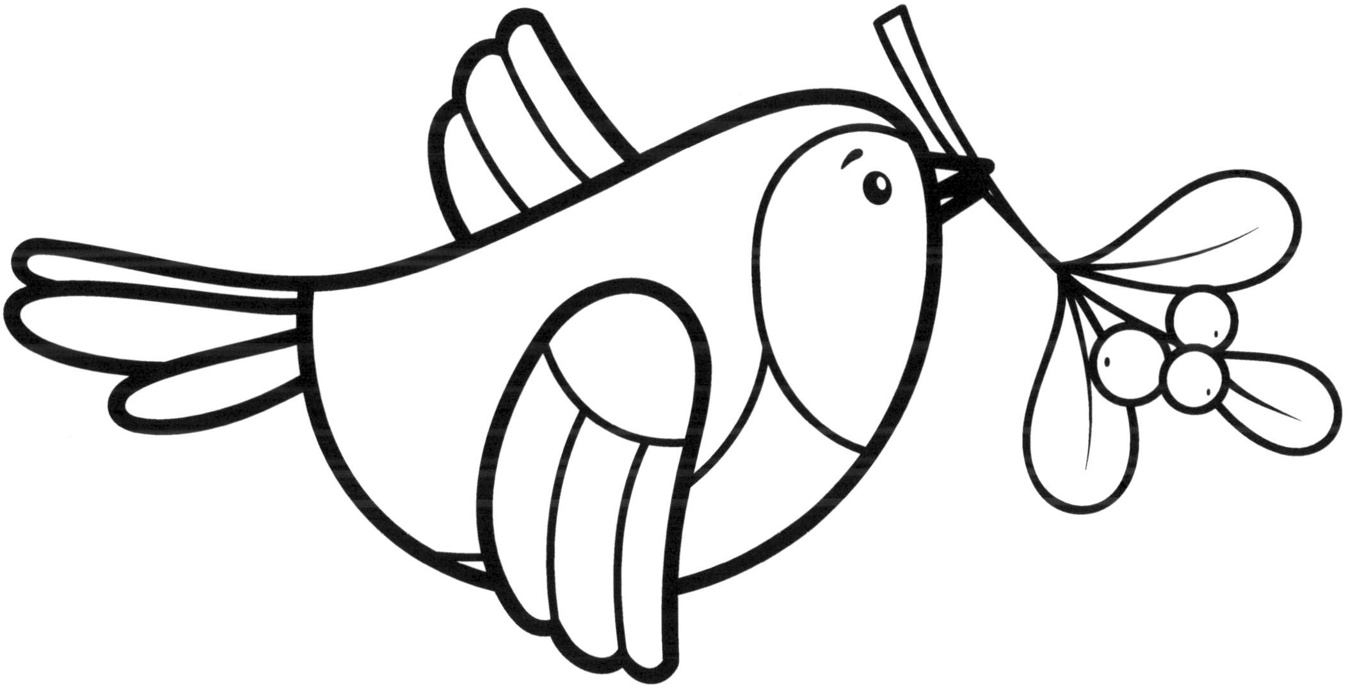

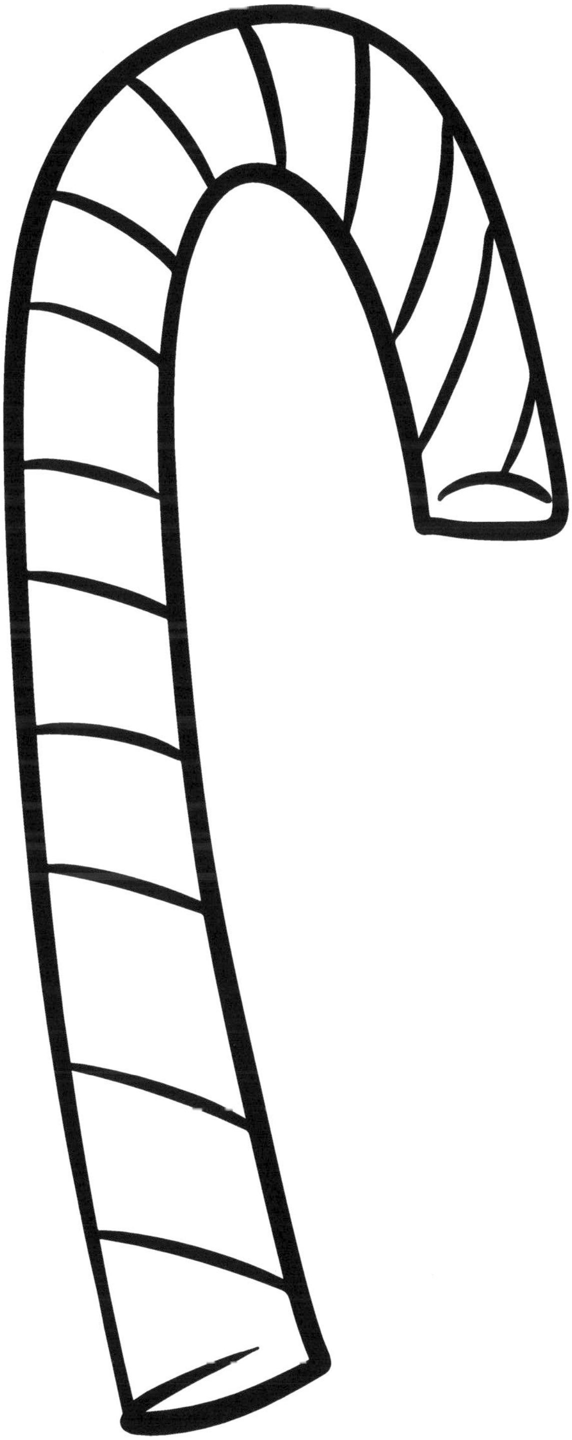

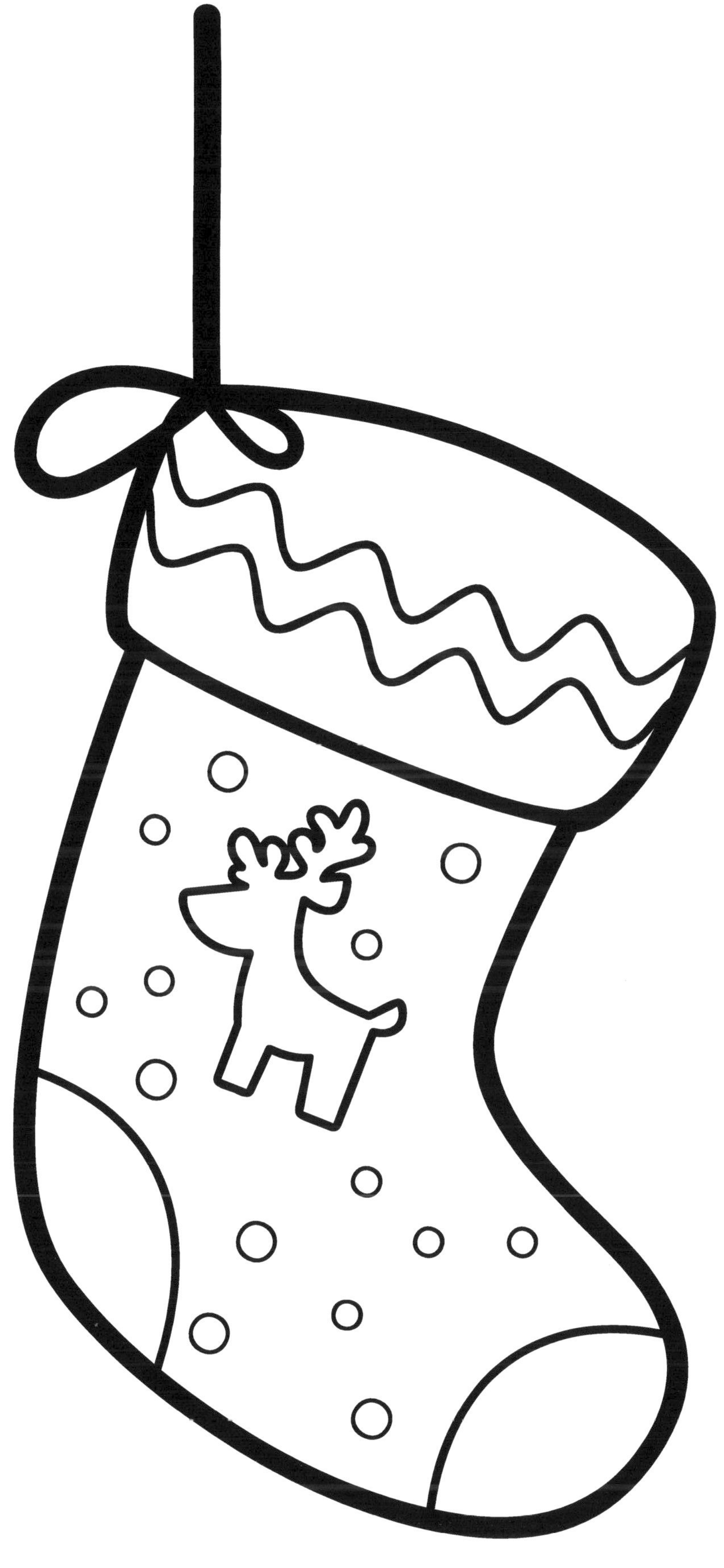

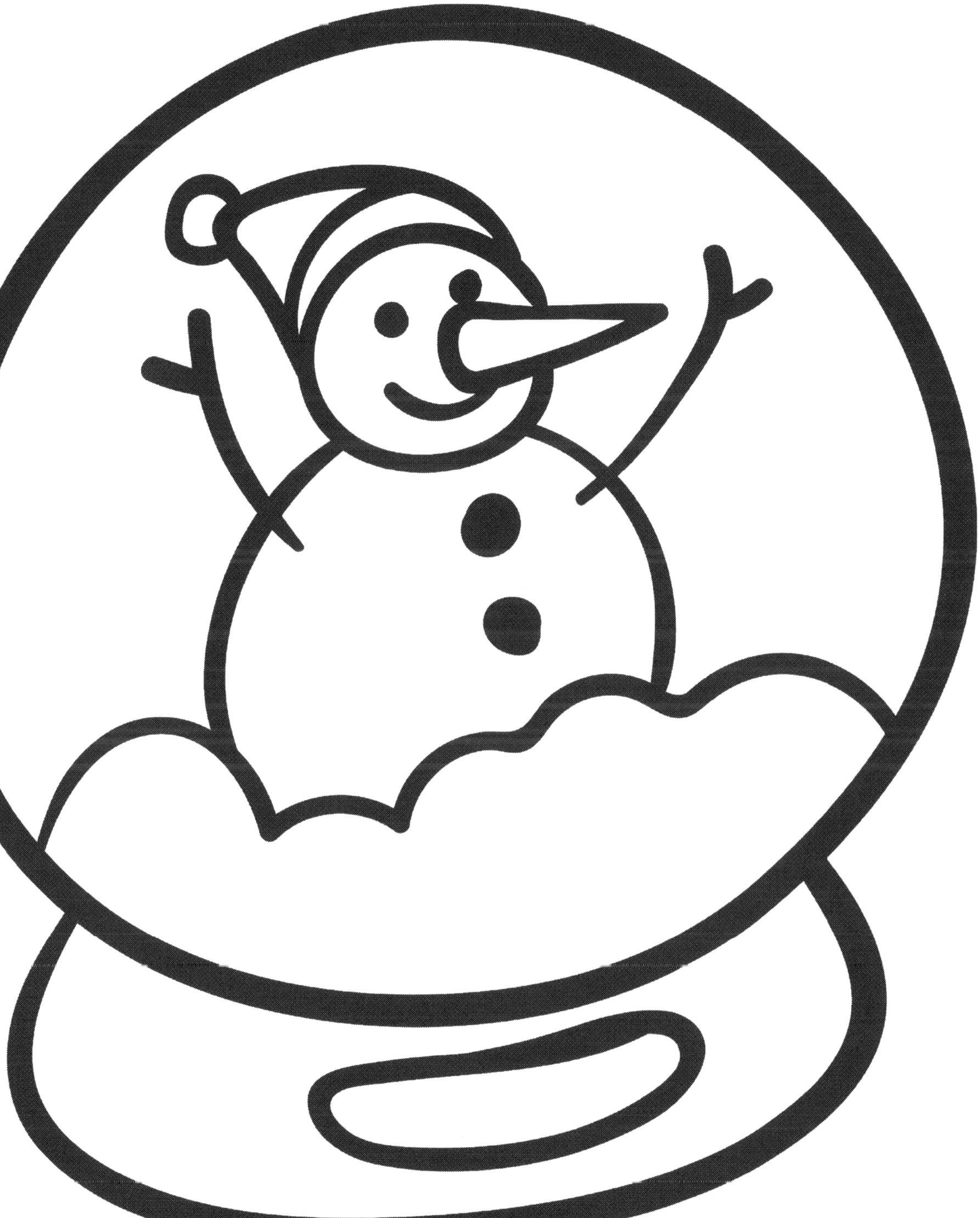

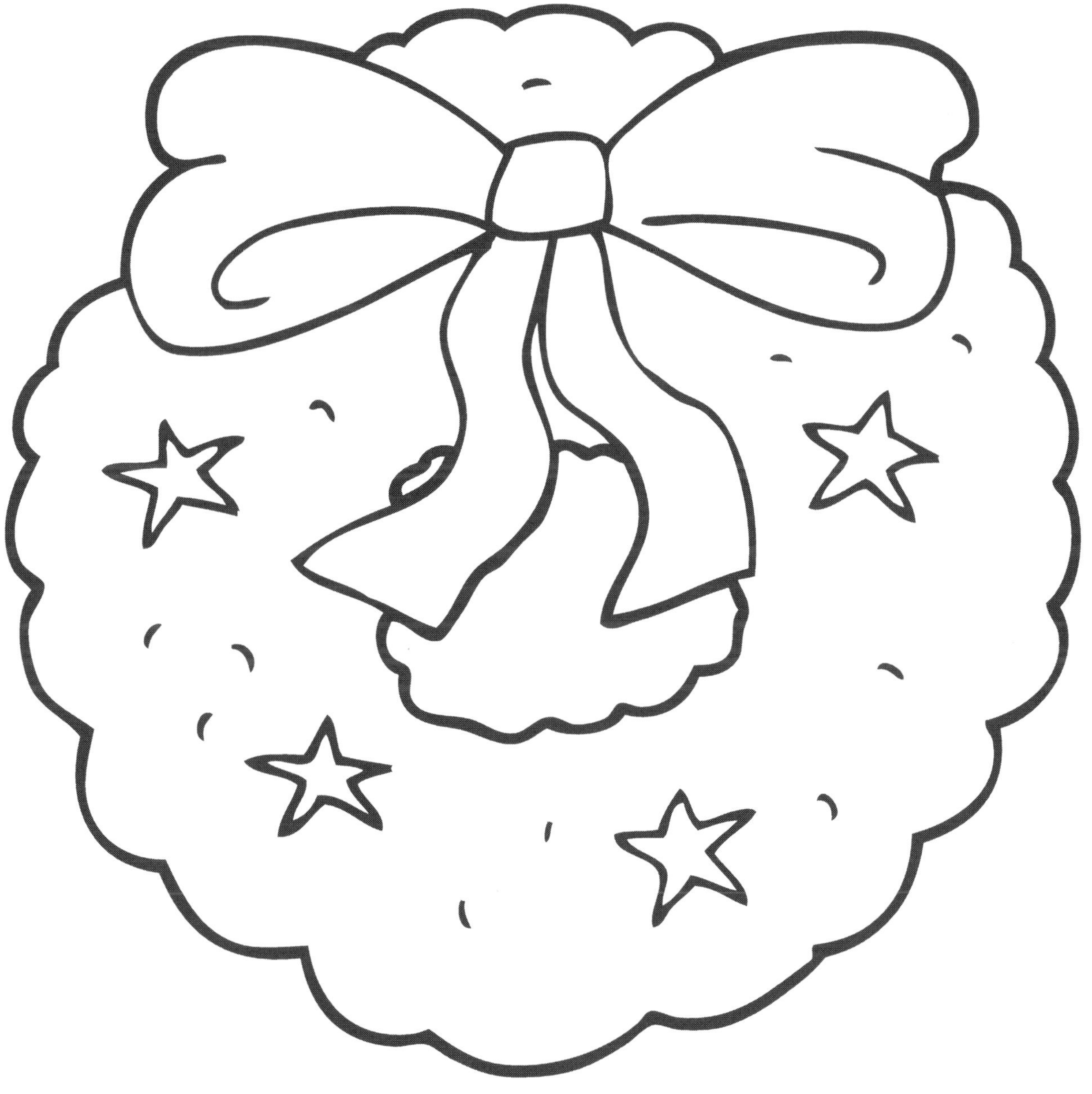

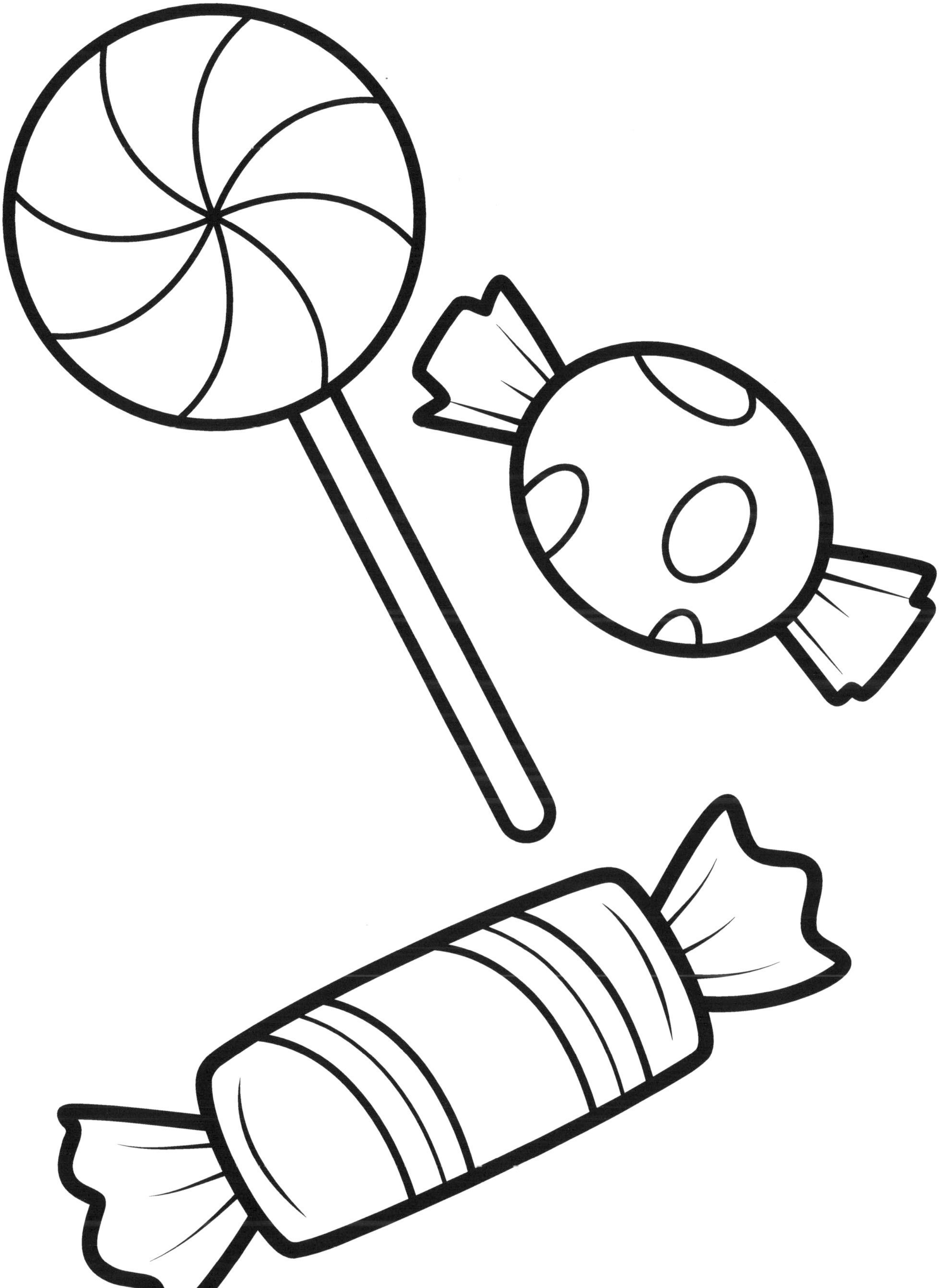

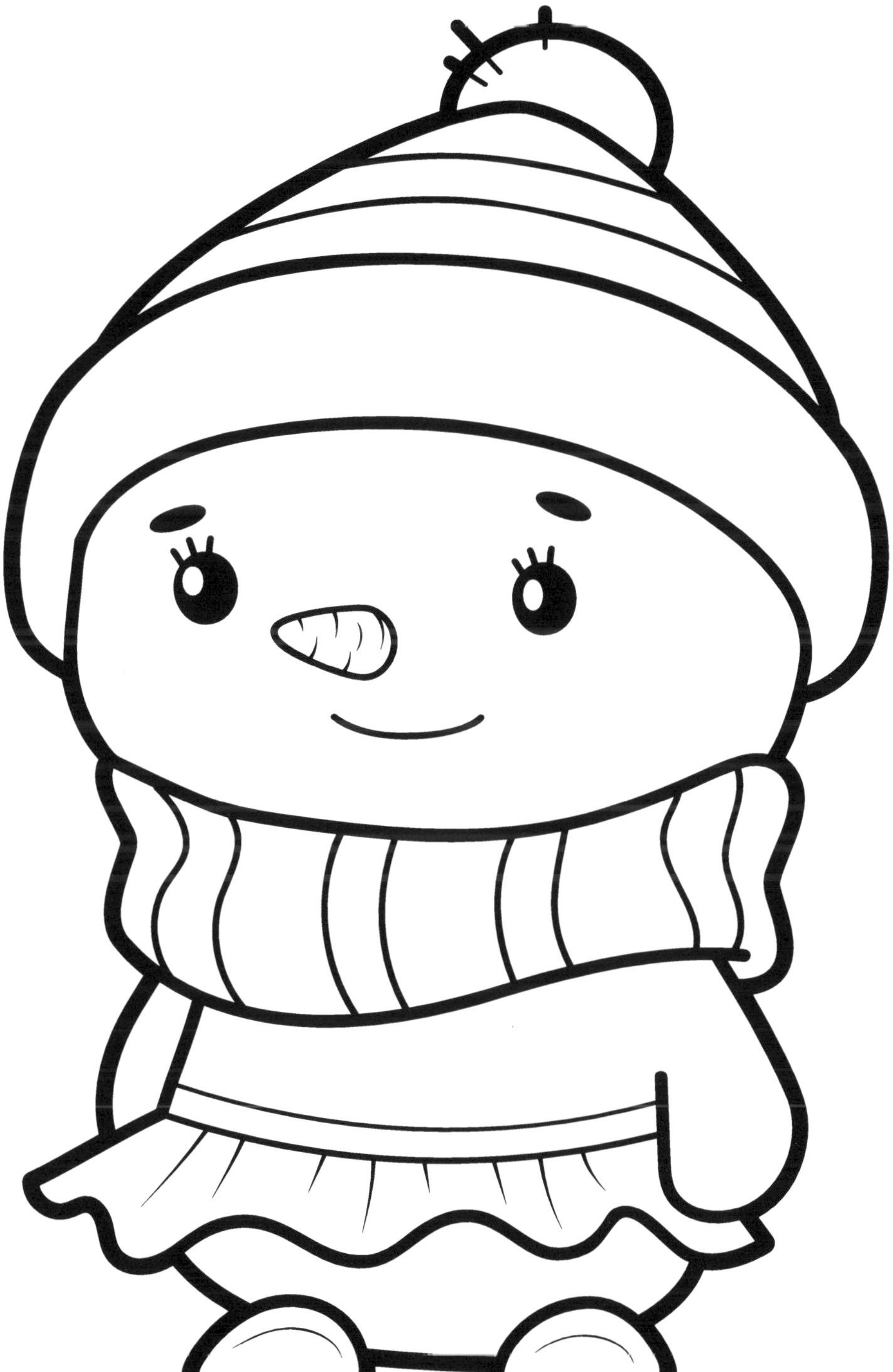

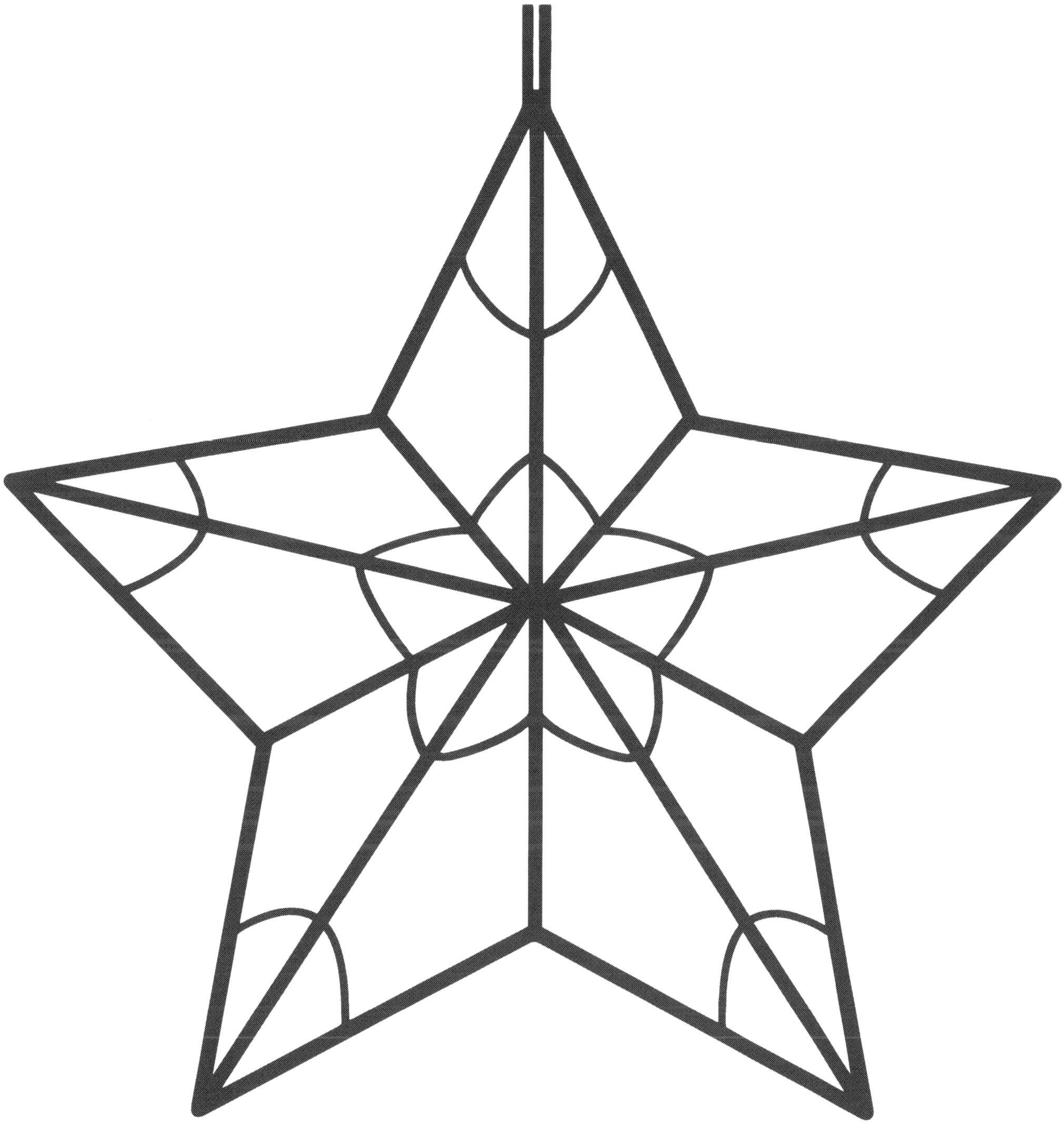

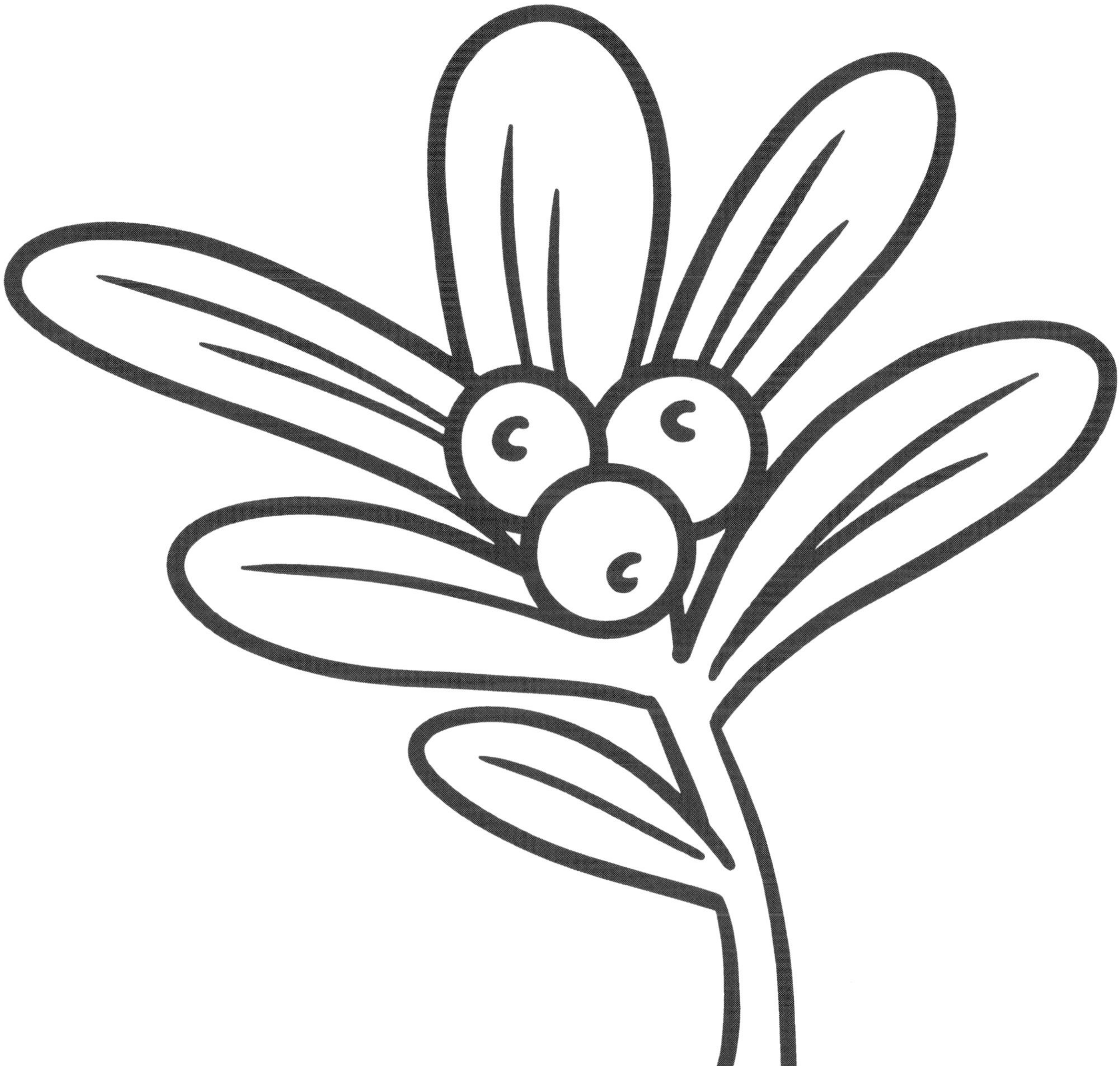

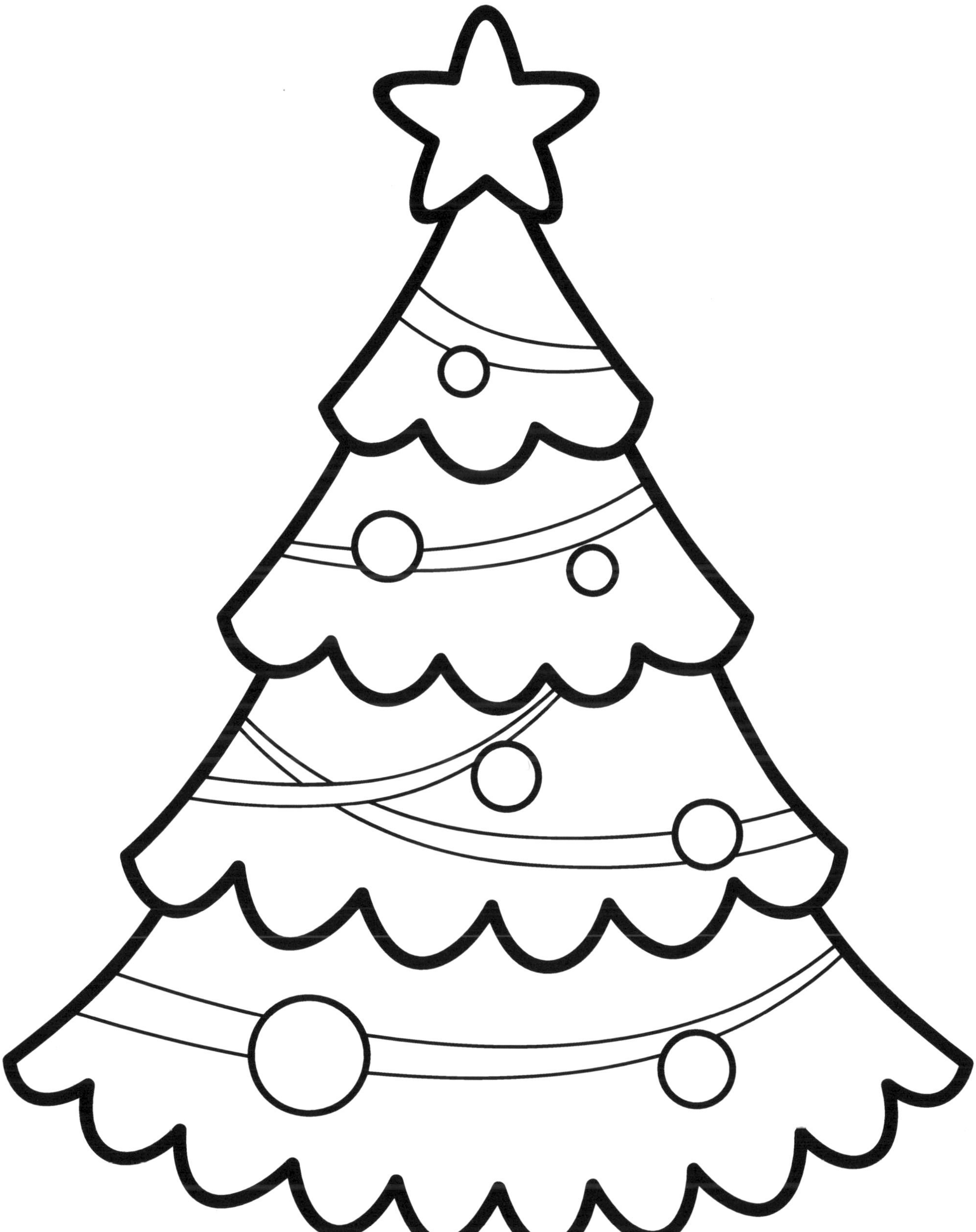

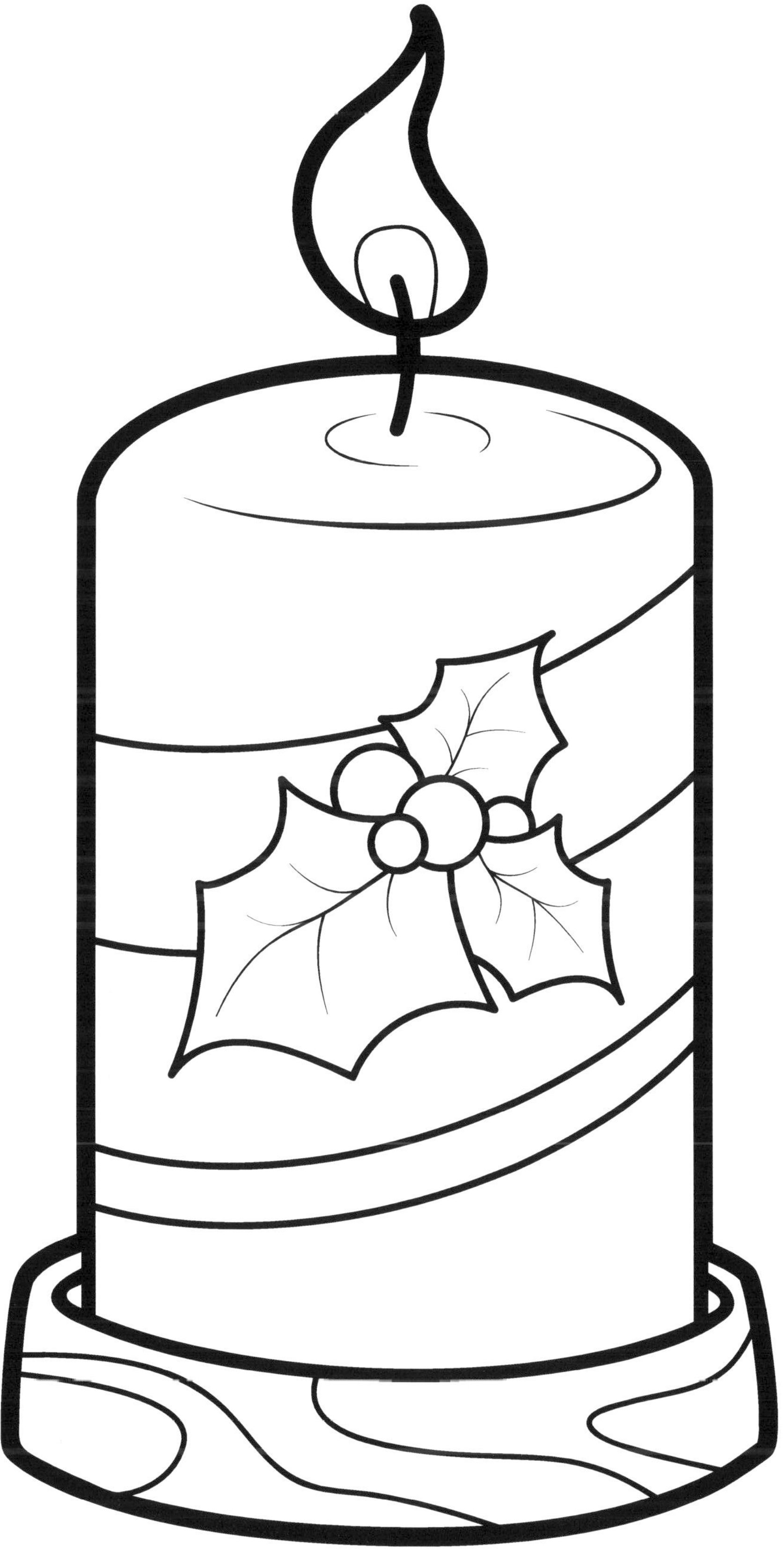

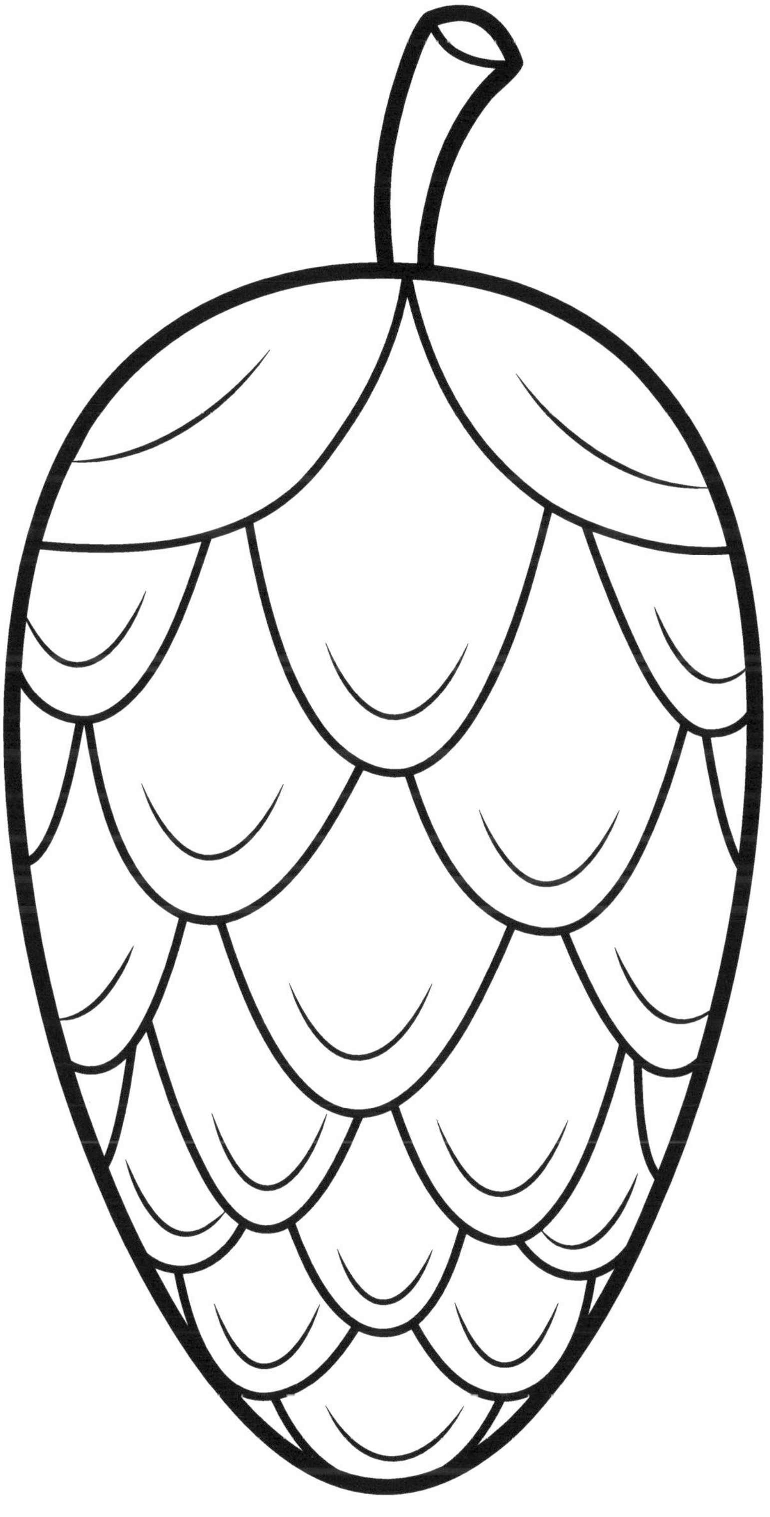

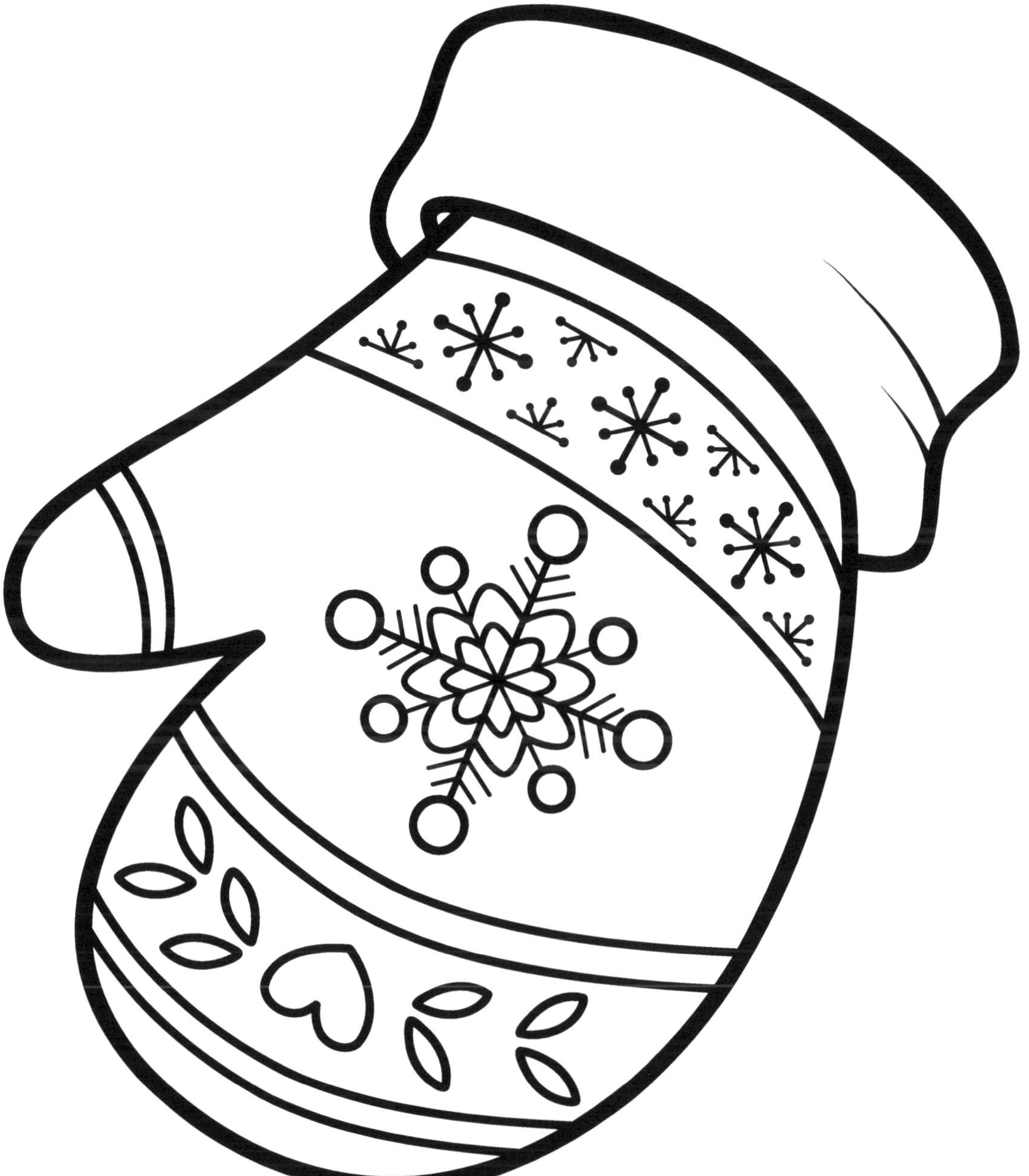

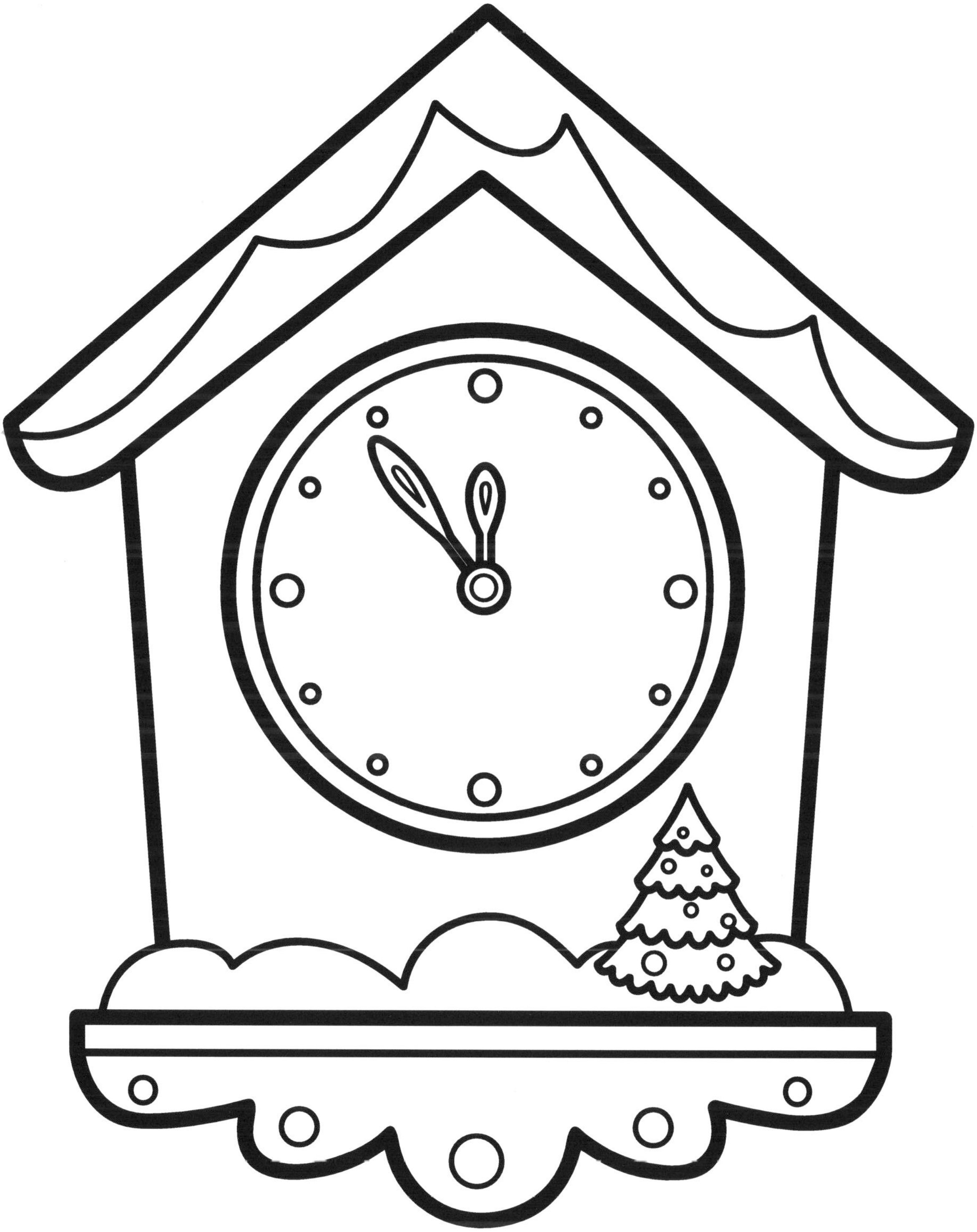

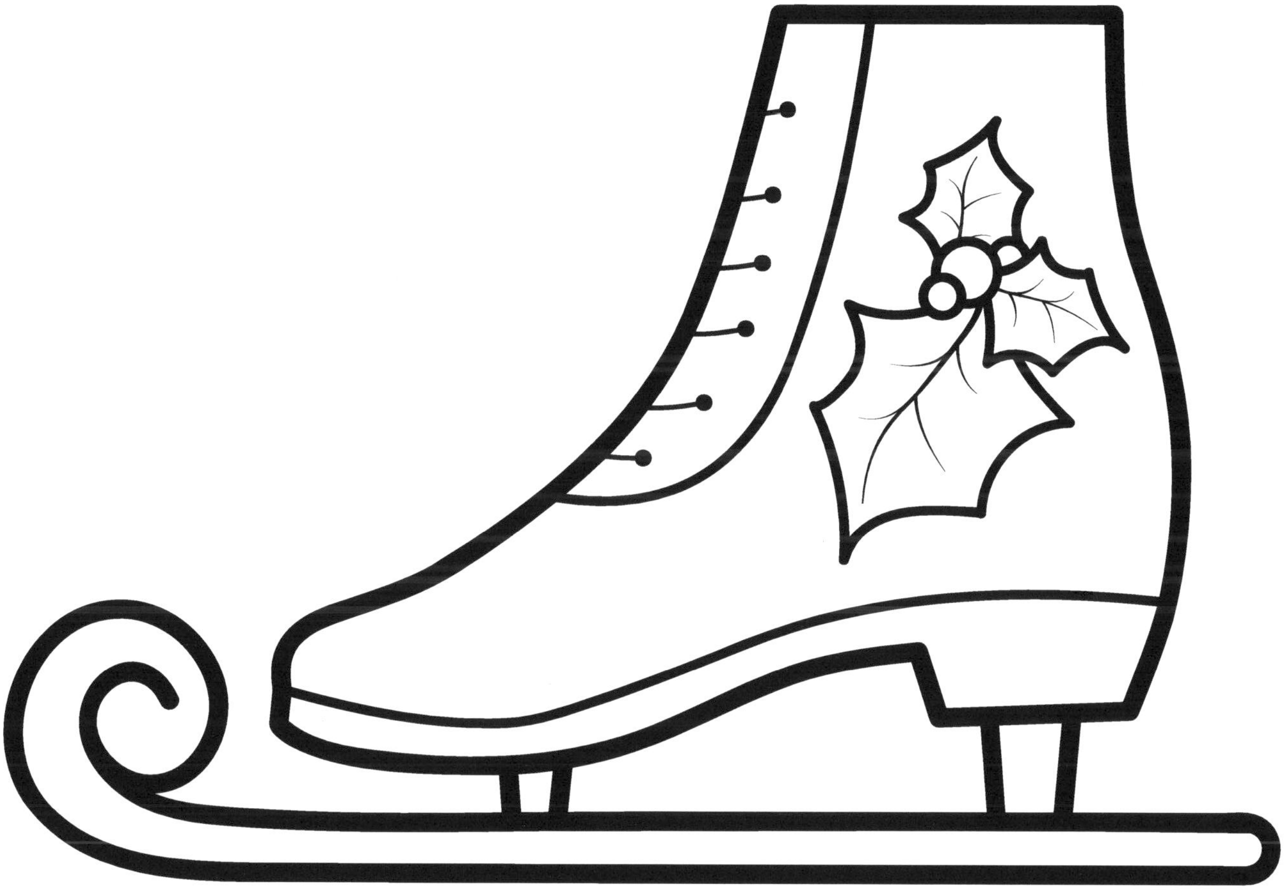

Printed in Great Britain
by Amazon

32391771R00035